Alexander Smith Faulkner

An Historical Sketch of the Naruka State of Ulwar in

Rajputana

Alexander Smith Faulkner

An Historical Sketch of the Naruka State of Ulwar in Rajputana

ISBN/EAN: 9783337013868

Printed in Europe, USA, Canada, Australia, Japan

Cover: Foto ©ninafisch / pixelio.de

More available books at **www.hansebooks.com**

AN

HISTORICAL SKETCH

OF THE

NARUKA STATE OF ULWAR

IN

RAJPUTANA

BY

ALEX. S. FAULKNER,

SURGEON-MAJOR, INDIAN MEDICAL SERVICE,

AND AGENCY SURGEON AT THE COURT OF ULWAR.

Calcutta:

THACKER, SPINK, AND CO.

1895.

PRINTED BY THACKER, SPINK, AND CO., CALCUTTA.

PREFACE.

FROM its very nature this work is necessarily a compilation, and in this respect extracts and facts have been freely borrowed from Mills' "History of India," Keene's "Moghul Empire," Powlett's "Gazetteer of Ulwar," Tod's "Annals of Rajasthan," and other authors.

The object, then, of this compilation has been to draw together, as it were, in a convenient form, facts connected with the History of the Ulwar State from many sources.

Notwithstanding its many imperfections, it is hoped this small volume will be of interest, at any rate, to those who are or have been connected with, or have reminiscences of a visit to, the Ulwar State.

ULWAR.

CONTENTS.

CHAPTER I.

CHAPTER I.

HISTORY OF THE ULWAR STATE.

THE Native State of Ulwar is situated in the northern portion of the province of Rajputana. It comprises an area of 3,000 square miles, and has a population of 759,417 according to the last Census. The State is bounded on the north by Gurgaon, and the native district of Kot Kasim, on the east by Mathura and Bhurtpore and on the south and west by Jeypore territory. The State derives its name as a whole, from the largest city in the State of that name, which existed before the foundation of the State, as an independent Principality.

The origin of the name of this city is probably derived, by an interchange of letters from the word Arbal, the name of the principal chain of Hills, with which those near the city are connected, and which form a portion of the Aravalli Range. The Nikumba Rajputs built the City and Fort of Ulwar. Another instance of a Nikumba Fort, in the State, is to be .seen at Indor near Tapookra.

Before giving a description of the foundation of the State, it will be convenient to specify here, the names and positions of the different tracts of country, which, or parts of which, are included in the Ulwar State, and which have an historical bearing on subsequent events.

The present territory comprising the Ulwar State was composed originally of five separate tracts of country, known as follows, *viz.*—(1) The Raht, (2) The Wal, (3) The Rajawat country, (4) Mewat, and (5) Portions of Narukhand, or the country of the Naruka Rajpoots.

(1) *The Raht country*—Is situated on the north-west border of the State. It is the country of the Chauhan Rajputs, who claim to be descendants of the famous Pirthwi Raj, king of Delhi. A Chauhan Rajput, named Madan is said to have founded Mandawar in this State in A.D. 1170. Another Chauhan Rajput named Halaji (fifth in descent from Madan) had three sons, *viz.*—

(i) Hansaji, whose grandson became a Mussulman, and received the title of Rao, and his direct descendant is the present Rao of Mandawar.

(ii) Khan Hardaoji, founded the family of Barod.

(iii) Rajdeoji, the youngest son, for some special services received the title of Raja, and he settled at Nimrana. At present Nimrana is regarded as a feudatory of Ulwar, and the Raja of Nimrana pays a certain tribute to the State.

(2) *The Wal country* is on the western border of the State, and was chiefly occupied by the Shekhawat Rajputs. Rai Mal, son of Shekhji, is said to have been the father of the Wal families in this State, thus :

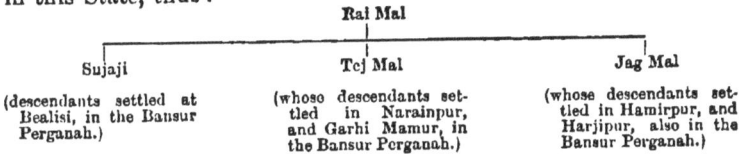

Rai Mal

Sujaji	Tej Mal	Jag Mal
(descendants settled at Bealisi, in the Bansur Perganah.)	(whose descendants settled in Narainpur, and Garhi Mamur, in the Bansur Perganah.)	(whose descendants settled in Hamirpur, and Harjipur, also in the Bansur Perganah.)

(3) *The Rajawat country* lies to the south-west of the State, and is a portion of the territory at one time in the possession of the once powerful Rajawat Rajputs, of Jeypore. They are descendants of Raja Bhagwant Singh, of Amer, and the tract of country over which they ruled corresponds to the Thana-Ghazi Perganah. Bhangargh was most probably their largest city, and at that place are still to be seen the ruins of their palaces and temples.

(4) *Mewat.*—All the remaining portion of the State (except Narukhand) is in Mewat, which comprises more than half of the Ulwar territory. The majority of the inhabitants of Mewat are called Meos. They are Mussulmans, but claim to be of Rajput origin. The most numerous of the Ulwar clan of Meos, are the Naies, the Singals, and the Dulotes.

(5) *Narukhand,* or the country of the Naruka Rajputs, comprises the tract of country to the south-east of the State. The history of Narukhand is so important, that it is necessary to trace in detail, the origin and subsequent history of the Naruka Rajputs, as they form the groundwork on which a history of the Ulwar State can be built.

CHAPTER II.

THE NARUKA RAJPUTS OF NARUKHAND.

In Sumbat 1424 (A.D. 1367) Ude Karan, the then head of Kutchawa Rajputs, took his seat on the Gadi of Amer, as Chief of the Jeypore territory. His eldest son was Bar Singh, who ought to have succeeded his father, but who resigned his right in that direction. A curious legend relates the cause which is assigned for this idiocrasy. It is stated that Bar Singh was to have married a certain lady, for whom his father, in jest, pretended to have a fancy. This gave great offence to Bar Singh, insomuch so that he insisted on his father taking his own place as bridegroom, and to any son who might be born of the marriage he resigned his right to the Gadi of Amer, after his father's death. Nahar Singh was the issue of the above marriage, and he consequently succeeded his father, whilst Bar Singh received an estate of 84 villages in the districts of Jhak and Mozabad, which are situated about 30 miles to the south-west of the city of Jeypore. Bar Singh had a son named Mairaj, who in his time had a son named Naru. From Naru descended the important clan of Rajputs, known as the Narukas of Narukhand

Naru had five sons, *viz.*, Lala, Dasa, Tejsi, Jeta, and Chitar.

Lala, the ancestor of the Lalawat Narukas, to which the Ulwar family belong.

Dasa, the ancestor of the Dasawat Narukas, to which the Chief of Uniara, and that of Lawa belong.

Tejsi, whose descendants had villages in Jeypore and the village of Hadirhera in the Ulwar State.

Jeta, whose descendants had Pipal-Khera, but who now have possessions in Jeypore.

Chitar, whose descendants hold a small jagir at Naitala-Kaikar in the Ulwar State.

Lala had a son named Ude Singh, who served under Bharat Mal, of Amer ; his son again, Lar Khan, served under the great Man Singh, and received his title of Khan from the Emperor of Delhi. It is, however, with Lar Khan's son, named Fateh Singh, in whom we are specially interested, as he was the first of the Lalawat Narukas who permanently settled in Narukhand, in the Ulwar State, at Macheri, near Rajgurgh.

Fateh Singh had the following issue, *viz.* :—

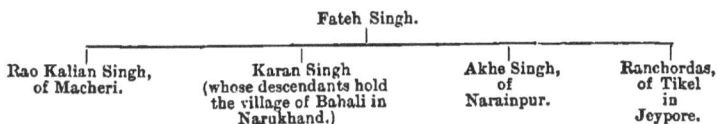

Fateh Singh.

| Rao Kalian Singh, of Macheri. | Karan Singh (whose descendants hold the village of Bahali in Narukhand.) | Akhe Singh, of Narainpur. | Ranchordas, of Tikel in Jeypore. |

In the following lines, it will not be necessary to refer again to the three younger sons, and our remarks will be confined alone to the eldest son, Rao Kalian Singh, and his descendants, as he was the ancestor, in a geneological sense, of the founder and subsequent Chiefs of the Ulwar State.

In not supporting his Chief, Jey Singh of Amer, against a rival, it seems Rao Kalian Singh lost the family estates of Jhak, and he was banished to Macheri, in Narukhand, a territory which was then in the hands of the Dasawat Narukas.

Rao Kalian Singh did not, however, remain long at Macheri, as he endeavoured to take possession of Kama in Bhurtpore territory, which had been bestowed on Sewai Jai Singh by Aurangzeeb. Being unsuccessful in this attempt, as one of Jai Singh's own sons succeeded his father in the possession of Kama, Rao Kalian Singh returned to Macheri in S. 1728 (A.D. 1671).

A local legend relates the reason which induced Rao Kalian Singh to return to Macheri. It is stated he solicitated directions from the widow of one Kherat Singh, just before she became "sati." She replied in the following lines :—

> * " Jao bas abdes men, Rao Kalian ap
> Age kul men honge, partap ik Partap."

---

* " Go, dwell in your own land Rao Kalian
Of your house will hereafter be the fortunate Partap."

Rao Kalian Singh had five sons, all of whom had issue, and it is interesting to note that they all had their respective estates in the Ulwar territory, as follows :—

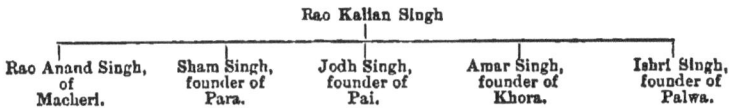

Rao Kalian Singh

Rao Anand Singh, of Macheri.	Sham Singh, founder of Para.	Jodh Singh, founder of Pai.	Amar Singh, founder of Khora.	Ishri Singh, founder of Palwa.

In regarding Rao Kalian Singh as the originator of the Ulwar State, under circumstances more of descent than of actual possession, it must be noted here, that his sons, who founded estates in the Ulwar territory, had, and their descendants still have, an important bearing in the destinies, and subsequent history of the State. They originated the "Panch Tikanas," which at the present day consist of Bijwar, Para, Pai, Khora, and Palwa. Their offshoots are known to this day as the "Bara Kotri," a term which was borrowed from Jeypore, where it is applied to the families who are the nearest relatives of the ruling Chief.

As the "Bara Kotri" in subsequent times had the honour and responsibility of assembling to determine which of two persons should be Chief of Ulwar, it is necessary to enumerate the Panch Tikanas in detail, giving the number of horses which they respectively furnish to the service of the State. A horse represents nearly 200 acres of cultivated land—

The Panch Tikanas :

Bijwar and its offshoots...	25	horses.
Para ,, ,, ,, ...	44	,,
Khora ,, ,, ,, ...	111½	,,
Palwa ,, ,, ,, ...	29½	,,
Pai ,, ,, ,, ...	13	,,

In tracing the genealogical tree of the present Chief of the Ulwar State, it will be necessary to refer to the five sons of Rao Kalian Singh , of Macheri.* Of these, Armand Singh, the eldest (who succeeded his father at Macheri), and Sham Singh (who founded the house of Para), are most intimately connected with our object. Rao Armand Singh's great grandson, Tej Singh, had two sons, *viz.*— Zorawar Singh, and Zalim Singh, and it was during their lifetime that the Macheri family was split in two. It was from the elder brother, Zorawar Singh, that the first recognised Chief of Ulwar, Maha Rao Raja Purtap Singh, was descended. Zalim Singh, the younger brother, founded the Bijwar family, which at the present time is included in the Panch Tikanas. Rao Kalian Singh's second son, Sham Singh, had two sons, *viz.* :—Nathu Singh, who succeeded his father at Para, and Madhu Singh, of Thana. Madhu Singh was the founder of the noble house of Thana, from which all the Chiefs of Ulwar, including the present Chief (with the exception of the first Chief) can trace their descent. It will thus be seen, and is no doubt a curious coincidence, that the first Chief of Ulwar has been the only one who is directly descended from Rao Kalian Singh's eldest son ; whilst all the remaining Chiefs have been descended directly from his second son, Sham Singh, of Para.

---

* *Vide* Genealogical tree, page 9.

GENEALOGICAL TREE OF THE PRESENT ULWAR CHIEF.

Rao Kalian Singh of Machori.

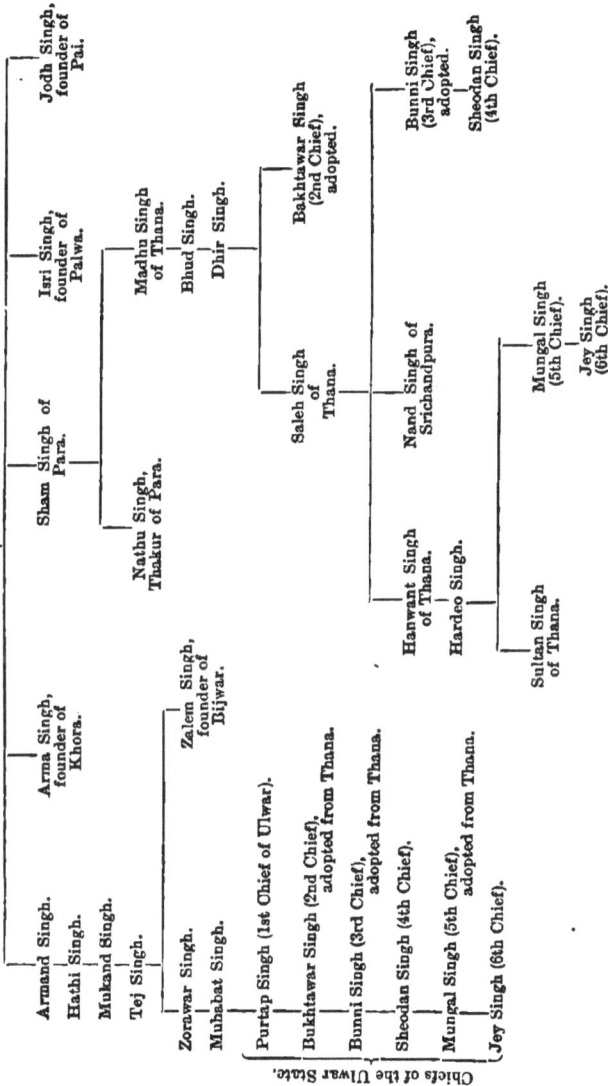

- Armand Singh.
- Hathi Singh.
- Mukand Singh.
- Tej Singh.

- Arma Singh, founder of Khora.
  - Zalem Singh, founder of Bijwar.
  - Zorawar Singh.
  - Mahabat Singh.
  - Purtap Singh (1st Chief of Ulwar).

- Sham Singh of Para.
  - Nathu Singh, Thakur of Para.

- Isri Singh, founder of Palwa.
  - Madhu Singh of Thana.
  - Bhud Singh.
  - Dhir Singh.
  - Saleh Singh of Thana.
    - Hanwant Singh of Thana.
    - Hardeo Singh.
    - Sultan Singh of Thana.
  - Bakhtawar Singh (2nd Chief), adopted.
    - Bunni Singh (3rd Chief), adopted.
    - Sheodan Singh (4th Chief).
  - Nand Singh of Srichandpura.
    - Mungal Singh (5th Chief).
    - Jey Singh (6th Chief).

- Jodh Singh, founder of Pai.

Chiefs of the Ulwar State:
- Purtap Singh (1st Chief of Ulwar).
- Bukhtawar Singh (2nd Chief), adopted from Thana.
- Bunni Singh (3rd Chief), adopted from Thana.
- Sheodan Singh (4th Chief).
- Mungal Singh (5th Chief), adopted from Thana.
- Jey Singh (6th Chief).

CHAPTER III.

HISTORY OF THE LIFE AND SOVEREIGNTY OF

MAHA RAO RAJA PURTAP SINGH.

1st CHIEF OF THE ULWAR STATE.

Ascended the Gadi A.D. 1753—*Died A.D.* 1791,

PURTAP SINGH was the son of Muhabat Singh and grandson of Zorawar Singh, and was born in A.D. 1740. After his father's death, he inherited as his sole birthright, two-and-a-half villages, situated in Narukhand in the Ulwar territory ; the villages being Macheri, Rajgargh, and half of Rampura.

Even up to the present day, he is often referred to as the " Arhai gaon ka Thakur."

It was then from such small beginnings that Purtap Singh completed the stupendous achievement, during his lifetime, of building up and establishing on a sound and lasting foundation an independent principality, which since his time has steadily increased in importance. His great name and actions, have naturally been handed down from one generation to another, and many local legends exist extolling his exceptional services, character, and chivalrous deeds.

In tracing a sketch of the life of Purtap Singh, it will be necessary, in the first instance, to make a passing reference to the contemporary history of his time, especially that which appertains to and is connected with the adjoining territories of Jeypore, Bhurtpore, Ulwar, and also to the Maharattas. In mentioning the name of Ulwar in this list, it must be remembered that Purtap Singh was, at the commencement of his successful career, known only as the Rao of Macheri and held his fief under Jeypore, and to him then Ulwar was a foreign principality in the Jat power.

At the commencement of his rule at Macheri, Raja Madhu Singh was Chief of Amer, and Purtap Singh's energy, address, and his physical prowess soon made him a prominent figure at the Court of Amer. One of his first important engagements, was to successfully carry out the orders of his Chief, to coerce his turbulent brethren, the Narukas of Uniara, whose peace with the Amer Chief was made by Purtap Singh.

On his return to Amer, the mutual feelings of friendship, which had up to this time always existed between himself and his Chief's Court, seem to have given way to those of fear and distrust; at any rate on the part of the Court, and Purtap Singh was no longer a *persona grata* at the Court of Amer.

Purtap Singh, however, was not kept inactive, and in S. 1822 (A.D. 1765) he was dispatched with the Jeypore troops to relieve the Fort of Ranthumbar (now called Madhupura), the imperial garrison of which was besieged by the Maharattas. It is asserted generally, that although the initial object of this expedition was the relief of the Fort, still a deep-seated wish and hope rested on the minds of Raja Madhu Singh, and his Court, that Purtap Singh would not return after this engagement.

They were, however, destined to disappointment so far as their wish was concerned, and Purtap Singh returned successful to Amer, after defeating the Maharattas.

After this second success in the service of his Chief, the feelings of jealousy became intensified, and he was looked up to with awe. About this time, an astrologer drew attention to the fact that there were rings or circles, around the pupils of Purtap Singh's eyes. As these were supposed to be, by the uninitiated, symbolical of kingly dignity, if not of royalty, the fact caused not only an aggravation of the feelings of jealousy, but also generated those of actual fear.

It was soon evident to the shrewd Purtap Singh that his presence at the Court of Amer was not encouraged, and finally he successfully frustrated a scheme, which had been planned to poison him, and he consequently lost no time and fled for his life and escaped to Bhurtpore.

Purtap Singh, nevertheless, always remained loyal to his Chief of Amer, and it is related that on his way to Bhurtpore, he halted at Rajgargh, one of his own villages, and enjoined his brethren to remain faithful to their Chief.

About A.D. 1766 he arrived at Bhurtpore and took service under Raja Jowahir Singh (son of the late powerful Jat Chief, Suraj Mal). Here he was received hospitably, and enjoyed the protection of the Bhurtpore Court. He was appointed administrator of a district, situated on the opposite banks of the Jumna, and was accompanied in his exile by his two faithful officials—Kooshialiram and Nundrum—both of whom greatly aided and abetted their master in all his ambitions.

Whilst Purtap Singh was thus employed, he was informed of the intention of his Bhurtpore Chief, to march his forces to Poshkar, through the Jeypore territory. To this event Purtap Singh owes his subsequent success, as this expedition was ultimately the indirect cause of his settling permanently at Macheri.

However, to follow this expedition, I will quote the following lines from Tod's " Rajasthan " :—

" Purtap Singh, of the Narooka clan, held the fief of Macheri ; for some fault he was banished the country by Madhu Singh, and fled to Jowahir Singh, from whom he obtained ' sirna ' (sanctuary) and lands for his maintenacne. The ex-chieftain of Macheri, though enjoying protection and hospitality at Bhurtpore, he did not the less feel the national insult, in that the Jat should dare thus unceremoniously to traverse their country. Whether the chief saw in this juncture an opening for reconciliation with his liege lord, or that a pure spirit of patriotism alone influenced him, he abandoned the place of refuge, and ranged himself at his old post, under the standard of Amber, on the eve of the battle, to the gaining of which he contributed not a little."

"For this opportune act of loyalty his past errors were forgiven, and Madhu Singh, who only survived that battle four days, restored him to his favour and his fief of Macheri."

Such, then, is the only recorded history of Purtap Singh's connection with this expedition, which resulted in the defeat of the Jats, at the battle of Maonda in S. 1825 (A.D. 1768).

Local legends, however, give a slightly different version,—1st, concerning the object of Raja Jowahir Singh's apparent march to Poshkar ; and 2ndly, concerning the conduct of Purtap Singh in deserting from the Jat army. When Purtap Singh first heard the news of the intended expedition, he volunteered his services to accompany it, and secretly in his own district, amassed a large sum of money for his own purposes, as he was really aware that the real object of the expedition was against Madhu Singh, of Jeypore. We are not here concerned what the reasons were for this expedition, but will confine our remarks to Purtap Singh. He accompanied

the Jat forces into Jeypore territory; and when all the final arrange-
ments had been made for the attack, all of which he knew, he, on
the eve of the battle went over to the Jeypore side, and naturally
they were greatly indebted to him for their ultimate success.

It was a marked trait in Purtap Singh's character, which was
exemplified in this instance, that he owed much of his success in
life to the fact that he always sided with the strongest side. Know-
ing the resources of the two armies, he wisely chose to throw in his
lot with the strongest, and here also an opportunity occurred to
give practical effect to his fore-thought in remaining loyal to his
own Chief, and on this occasion he made the most of his opportunities.

Although through the instrumentality of Purtap Singh the
Kutchawas were victorious, yet the battle of Maonda was a very
disastrous event for the Jeypore State, as the conflict was so desperate, that almost every chieftain of note on the Jeypore side was
killed, and this fact, culminating in the early death of the Chief himself after the battle, marks a point from which the Kutchawa power
temporarily declined.

As a reward for his services, Madhu Singh restored Purtap
Singh to his fief of Macheri, and conferred on him the title of Rao Raja.

On returning to Macheri, Rao Raja Purtap Singh assumed complete and independent authority, and very soon began to make his
power felt in the surrounding Naruka country.

A short reference must now be made to affairs at Jeypore which were not in a satisfactory condition. After Madhu Singh's death, shortly after the battle of Maonda, he was succeeded by Pirthi Singh II, under the guardianship of the mother of his younger brother Purtap Singh, and a long minority with its accustomed anarchy prevailed. Taking advantage of this state of affairs in Jeypore, Purtap Singh of Macheri began in earnest, to lay the foundation stones of the important principality, of which he was destined to be the founder. In S. 1827 (A.D. 1770) he built forts at Tehla and Rajpur. In S. 1828 (A.D. 1771) he completed the large fort at Rajgargh. In S. 1829 (A.D. 1772) he strengthened the fort at Malakhera, and in the following two years he built forts at Baldeogargh, Purtapgargh, Kankwari, Thana Ghazi, and at Ajabgargh, all in the south-west of the Ulwar territory.

On the other hand, he is said to have purposely discouraged cultivation, so as his country could offer no temptation to an invader, and to have no crops and fields inviting the encampment of large bodies of troops.

In S. 1830 (A.D. 1773) the Ulwar Fort was occupied by the Jats of Bhurtpore, and Nawal Singh was at the time Killadar of the Fort. The pay of the garrison was 15 months in arrears, and they were reduced to great straits. At the time Purtap Singh was at Kankwari, he was invited to take possession of the Fort of Ulwar on the condition that he paid the garrison what was due to them.

To this request he complied, and in S. 1830 he took possession of Ulwar City.

In S. 1832 (A.D. 1775) he took possession of the Fort of Ulwar, where the Jat garrison were interned. I cannot find any authority to quote, as to the means he made use of to gain an entrance to and occupy the Fort. Undoubtedly there was no bloodshed in the attainment of his object.

A local legend states, that Purtap Singh stipulated that as each man of the garrison left the Fort (and received his due,) one of his own men should enter, and take his place in the Fort. This arrangement having been agreed to on each side, the first man of the garrison made his exit, and before the rest received his pay, and was duly conducted down to the city. Here the money was taken from him, and he was made a prisoner. The money was then sent again to the Fort, and the second and succeeding men were all treated in a like manner. In the meanwhile, as each man of the garrison left the Fort, he was replaced by one of Purtap Singh's own men, who in this way ultimately occupied and took possession not only of the Fort but the whole garrison.

From this time Purtap Singh gained authority and respect, and was recognised by his brethren as their Chief, to whom they began to do homage, and present *nazars*. One man, however, refused to accept Purtap Singh's authority. This was Sarup Singh, probably the principal Dasawat Naruka, in Narukhand, and who owned the forts of Ramgargh and Taur (now Lachmangargh).

Purtap Singh, who apparently was never at a loss for some device to satisfy his thirst for extended authority and power, sent a man, named Andha Naik, and a party to Sarup Singh, on the pretence that they had deserted from Purtap Singh's camp. Andha Naik, thus gaining admission to Taur, made Sarup Singh a prisoner and brought him to Ulwar. As he still refused to present his *nazar*, he was put to death in a cruel way. Strips of wetted buffalo hide were bound round his head, which, slowly contracting as they dried, burst his skull. Purtap Singh also took possession of Sarup Singh's forts at Ramgargh and Lachmangargh.

Between S. 1832 (A.D. 1775) and S. 1839 (A.D. 1782) he further added a number of other places to his possessions, which were then in the hands of the Jats, *viz.*:—Bahadarpur, Dehra Jhindoli, Bansur, Behror, Barod, Rampur, Harsaura, Gadhi-Mamur and Thana-Ghazi.

About this time Purtap Singh was busy in other directions. In S. 1832 (A.D. 1775) Meerza Nasaf Khan was the Commander of the Imperial Troops of the Emperor of Delhi, and aided by the Maharattas, he proceeded to expel the Jats from the city of Agra, and subsequently attacked them in their own stronghold at Bhurtpore. Raja Newal Singh was at that time the Jat Chief, and Purtap Singh, continuing to carry out his old policy of siding with the strongest side, united his troops with those of Meerza Nasaf Khan.

Tod, in his " Annals of Rajasthan," states, with reference to this action, that " this timely succour and his subsequent aid in defeating the Jats obtained for him (Purtap Singh) the title of Rao Raja, and a *sannad* for Macheri, to hold direct of the Crown." He also received the much-coveted insignia, called "Mahi Maratib," which to the present day are only paraded on great occasions and festivals, and are preserved with great care by the Ulwar Durbar.

It is important to note that the granting of this *sanad* and title severed Macheri from Jeypore for ever.

To revert to Purtap Singh's relations with Meerza Nasaf Khan, Keene, in his " Moghul Empire," states that in A.D. 1779 " Meerza Nasaf Khan remained in contemptuous repose at Agra, only interrupted by a short and successful dash at some Rajpoot malcontents."

These remarks have reference to Purtap Singh, but it is difficult to obtain an accurate account as to the reasons of Purtap Singh's differences with Meerza Nasaf Khan at this time.

They were most probably due to the intrigues of the two brothers, Kushaliram Haldea and Doulat Ram, who were both at one time in Purtap Singh's service.

A local legend relates how and under what circumstances the two forces met, as follows :—

" Purtap Singh had by mistake shot a calf whilst out on a shooting expedition, and to cleanse himself of this outrage against his own religion, he decided to bathe in the Ganges. He determined to go in full state, accompanied by the flower of his army, combined with all the pomp and splendour of his Court.

On his return march he was surprised by Meerza Nasaf Khan's forces, and they met at Rassia, in Bhurtpore in S. 1836 (A.D. 1779). Here a desperate battle was fought, resulting in the total defeat of Purtap Singh's troops, and the loss of all his wealth and Court trophies.

Purtap Singh, however, with such of his followers who could break through, escaped to Lachmangargh, which was besieged for several months and ultimately abandoned.

The Rassia attack is commemorated locally in an ironical couplet, *viz.* :—

> * " Rassia Wali Dungri tujh ko sat salaam,
> Ure Kasumbi pagri, lajja rakhe Ram."

After his defeat Purtap Singh returned to Ulwar and had to re-plenish his coffers by plundering the towns of Baswa and Thana Ghazi.

In S. 1849 (A.D. 1792), Maharajah Purtap Singh, of Jeypore, marched his troops against Rajgargh, but returned unsuccessful to Jeypore.

---

* " Oh ! Rassia Hill seven times salaams,
Their red turbaue flew off, may Ram save their honor."

Two years before his death, Purtap Singh decided by a curious arrangement whom he should adopt as his heir, as he had no children of his own.

All the children, who were boys, and belonged to the " Bara Kotri," were summoned before him, a number of toys and sweets were arranged about the room, and each boy was to choose what he most fancied. A lad named Bukhtawar Singh chose a dagger and shield, and this so pleased the Rajput Chief, that he was declared to be his adopted heir.

Purtap Singh died in S. 1848 (A. D. 1791), the cause of death being a disease known as the fungus disease of India.

The following is a list of the perganahs which Purtap Singh possessed at the time of his death *viz.* : —

Ulwar, Malakhera, Rajgargh, Rajpur, Lachmangargh, Govind-gargh, Pipal-Khera, Ramgargh, Bahadarpur, Dehra, Tindoli, Hasaura, Behror, Barod, Bansur, Rampur, Hajipur, Hamirpur, Narainpur, Gahi-Mamur, Thana-Ghazi, Pertabgargh, Ajabgargh, Baldeogargh, Tehla, Khuntela, Titarpur, all in the Ulwar territory, and the following in Jeypore territory, *viz.* :—Sital, Gudha, Dubbi, Sikrai, and Baori-Khera.

In concluding this brief outline of the actions of this great man one is impelled to take a glance at the character of an individual who, under so many and trying circumstances, was able, nevertheless, to distinguish himself amongst his contemporaries.

From his own actions one trait of character is revealed, and that is his own personal ambition, combined with a love of authority, and command. He was endowed with great physical strength, a no mean qualification for success in the days in which he lived, and otherwise he was a shrewd, thoughtful, far-seeing man, who never lost a favourable opportunity, and always sided with the strongest side.

CHAPTER IV.

LIFE AND SOVEREIGNTY OF MAHA RAO RAJA SEWAEE BUKHTAWAR SINGH, BAHADUR,

2ND CHIEF OF THE ULWAR STATE.

Ascended the Gadi A.D. 1791—*Died A.D.* 1815.

––––––––

BUKHTAWAR SINGH was the son of Dhir Singh, and a direct descendant of Madhu Singh, who founded the House of Thana. He was placed on the *gadi* on the doctrine of adoption, the curious proceedings relative to which have already been recorded.

One of the first most important events after his accession, was his visit to Marwar in S. 1850 (A.D. 1793) on the occasion of his betrothal, to the daughter of the Thakur of Kuchawan. On his return to Ulwar, he visited Jeypore, but he was not, however, permitted to recover his liberty and return to his own capital till he had resigned the Forts of Sital, Gudha, Dubbi, Sikrai and Baora-Khera.

On his return to Ulwar, Bukhtawar Singh's attentions were directed towards Bhurtpore territory, and he took possession of

Kama and its adjacent perganahs, on the pretext that they formed part of the jagir of his ancestor Rao Kalian Singh.

The Maharattas at this time were a great power in Hindustan, and Diwan Ram Sewak, who was formerly in Purtap Singh's service, gave trouble, especially in his endeavours to side with the Maharattas against his present Chief, with whom he had quarrelled, and under Bukhtawar Singh's orders, this unfaithful servant was put to death.

Grant Duff, in describing the Maharattas at this time, between A.D. 1803 and 1806, says : " Originally their great strength consisted in their cavalry, capable of any amount of endurance, able to subsist without a commissariat, without tents, without organization. Taking with them but sufficient for the provision of the day, a spare blanket, and a spare horse, they subsisted on the country through which they passed, until a great victory or some unlooked-for prize gave them the opportunity of loading themselves with plunder." Undoubtedly a formidable foe to meet, and Bukhtawar Singh so appreciated this fact that he professed himself willing to accept the protection of the British Government (as represented then by the Honourable East India Company), and he concluded with them a treaty of offensive and defensive alliance.

He was rewarded for his loyalty by the transfer to himself of Kama, which had been forfeited by the Raja of Bhurtpore. To suit his own convenience, as Kama was separated from his own territory, Bukhtawar Singh was permitted to exchange Kama for Kishengargh and its adjacent perganahs.

To revert now in more detail, to Bukhtawar Singh's connection with the British Government against the Maharattas, it will be necessary, in the first instance, to make a passing reference to General, Lord Lake, the then Commander-in-Chief in India. It will be remembered how well Lord Lake carried out the policy of Lord Wellesley, Governor-General in India, " to break for ever the power of the Maharatta confederacy," with a recollection of his glorious victories at Coël, Alligargh, Delhi, Agra, and at Laswaree.

It is with the latter battle that we are now most concerned. Lord Lake marched at the head of three Regiments of Dragoons, five of Native Cavalry, one European Infantry Regiment (the 76th), and four battalions of sepoys in pursuit of the Maharattas. He came up with the enemy at Laswaree. Here they were strongly posted, their right thrown back on a rivulet, the banks of which were extremely difficult of access, their left rested on the village of Laswaree, whilst their entire front (which lay concealed from view by long grass) was defended by a most formidable line of artillery. They were commanded by Abajer, a Maharatta, and officered entirely by natives.

Major Thorn in describing the actual battle says : " From the commencement of the conflict, early in the morning to the close of the general action in the evening, the enemy discovered a firmness of resolution and contempt of death which could not fail to command the admiration of their opponents, whose energies in the struggle were strained to the utmost, though nothing could repress their ardour or withstand the impetus of their united exertions. The enemy fought with great determination and did not quit the field of battle until they were actually driven from every position and had lost every gun."

Thus terminated the glorious victory of Laswaree on November 1st, 1803, probably the most desperate battle in which the British troops had been engaged against the powerful Maharattas.

This great battle, affecting as it did the permanent British relations with the Ulwar State, and also to a great extent with the neighbouring States, was an event most important to Rajputana.

Thorn states that: " On the 19th December 1803, a treaty of defensive alliance was concluded by the Commander-in-Chief with the Raja of Macheree. His capital or stronghold is Ulwar and from the local situation and resources of this Chief, he had it in his power to impede or repel every incursion of the Maharattas into the northern parts of Hindustan."

On this occasion Bukhtawar Singh's shrewd vakeel, Ahmed Buksh Khan, rendered most valuable aid to Lord Lake in procuring supplies for his army and in sending a small force from Ulwar to co-operate with the British troops, and further in giving information of the movements and strength of the Mahrattas, all of which greatly tended to help Lord Lake in his great victory.

For these services, the British Government conferred Ferozpur in Gurgaon on Ahmed Buksh Khan, and Bukhtawar Singh out of his own grant gave him Lahura in Hariana, which was made independent of Ulwar.

The Chief himself was not forgotten; the district called Raht, in the north-west of the State, and Hariana, and a portion of Mewat were conferred on him. Also in 1805 he received from the British Government Tijara, and Tapookra, in the north-east of the State and he was permitted to exchange Hariana, for the Perganahs of Katumbar and Sunkra.

The next important event in Bukhtawar Singh's sovereignty, took place a year or two later. A great inter-statal war was on the point of bursting out in Rajputana. It was indeed a plot to depose Raja Maum, of Jodhpore, in favour of one Dhonkal Singh, a Pretender. At the time Rae Chund was prime minister of Jeypore, and with the object of forwarding his Chief's views for the hand of Princess Kisnna Komari, daughter of Rana Bhim Singh, of Udaipur (more popularly known as "Kishna Komari Bai, Flower of Rajasthan") he supported the cause of the Pretender. It is not our purpose to follow the leading actors in their exploits, at this interesting and romantic juncture in the history of Rajputana, but it was necessary to refer to the unsettled state of Jeypore at this time, in connection with the subsequent actions of Bukhtawar Singh, who so interfered with the affairs of the Jeypore State, that he attracted the attention of the British Government, by whom he was compelled to sign a treaty " to bind himself not to enter into negotiations or engagements with other Chiefs."

Nevertheless in A.D. 1812, Bukhtawar Singh again took possession of the forts which he had to resign when he first visited Jeypore (*vide* page 23), this act being a breach of the treaty he had lately made with the British Government, and as he refused to give them up, it was decided to send a small British force to Ulwar, to compel Bukhtawar Singh to acquiesce, and it was not till they were within sight of the Ulwar Fort, that Bukhtawar Singh was persuaded by his advisers to surrender these Forts to Jeypore. He also had to pay all the expenses of the British expedition.

A few years later, it was apparent that Bukhtawar Singh's mind was deranged, and his insanity took a peculiar form, his hatred of Mussulmans being its chief characteristic. Some extraordinary stories are told of his mad doings at this time, and the origin of this hatred for Mussulmans seems to have been his animosity against his former official and friend, Ahmed Buksh Khan, who in reality had done him such excellent service.

It is a curious point to note, merely as a coincidence, that in after years, Bukhtawar Singh was succeeded by a Chief whose tendencies strongly inclined towards Mussulmans.

Bukhtawar Singh died from the effects of his disease in A.D. 1815.

The sovereignty of Bukhtawar Singh is especially important from the fact that the British Government made their first treaty with the Ulwar State during his tenure of rule.

CHAPTER V.

LIFE AND SOVEREIGNTY OF MAHA RAO RAJA SEWAEE BUNNI SINGH, BAHADUR.

3RD CHIEF OF THE ULWAR STATE

Ascended the Gadi A.D. 1815—*Died A.D.* 1857.

In the perusal of the records of this reign, its most noticeable point seems to be the marked tendency towards, if not an actual progress in, the civilization of the State. Wars and constant fighting, intrigues of races, and the din of turmoil and strife, give way to a more peaceful condition of affairs, by an attempt to introduce a system of administration, by means other than by the use of the sword.

Bunni Singh was born in A.D. 1808, and was the third son of Saleh Singh, of Thana, who was Maha Rao Raja Bukhtawar Singh's elder brother. His accession to the *gadi* was disputed from the first, as Bukhtawar Singh, like his predecessor, left no legitimate son. Before his death, however, Bukhtawar Singh had openly adopted

Bunni Singh as his heir, but his right to the *gadi* was contested by Bulwant Singh, who was Bukhtawar Singh's illegitimate son and was a year younger than Bunni Singh.

Although Bunni Singh was accepted as their Chief by the Rajputs generally, still they had a powerful contingent headed by the famous Ahmed Buksh Khan, who supported Bulwant Singh's claims. Emissaries were sent by both parties to the Resident at Delhi, who compromised these political matters for the time being by sending killats to each aspirant, and arranged that Bunni Singh should have the title, whilst Bulwant Singh exercised the power of the State.

This arrangement was sanctioned by the British Government, and when Bunni Singh took his seat on the *gadi*, Bulwant Singh was allowed to sit beside him on his left side.

Both claimants, however, being minors, the administration of the State was conducted for the next nine years by Diwans, amidst constant wrangles between the rival parties. This unsatisfactory state of things lasted till A.D. 1824, when a sanguinary fight took place between the two parties in Ulwar, which resulted in a victory for Bunni Singh, who made his adversary, Bulwant Singh, a prisoner. After this event the British Government decided that Bunni Singh should settle a jagir on Bulwant Singh, but he openly declined to do so. As this open rebellion had to be checked, advantage was taken of the opportunity to order the small British force which was sent against Bhurtpore to march on to Ulwar. The object of the expedition was attained without bloodshed, and Bunni Singh was compelled to make a provision for Bulwant Singh, partly in land and partly in money, the both combined to be equivalent to the value of the lands ceded to Ulwar by the British Government in Bukhtawar Singh's reign (*vide* page 27.)

In A.D. 1826 Bulwant Singh was consequently released and proceeded to Tijara, which now became his own property. His life here seems to have been uneventful, but he left a good reputation in the country he ruled for 19 years. His great work, which still exists, was the construction of a Fort, on a conspicuous hill to the east of the town. Bulwant Singh, however, did not live to see his work completed, as he died childless in A.D. 1845 and all his possessions reverted to the Ulwar State.

To revert to Bunni Singh.

He certainly had not succeeded to a peaceable inheritance, for his people at the time are described as " singularly savage and brutal, robbers by profession, never to be reformed or subdued," but nevertheless, he accomplished the difficult task of bringing them into a condition of comparative order and submission. The Meos were the most troublesome of his subjects in this respect, and it was not till after the infliction of signal chastisement, by burning their villages and carrying off their cattle, that he succeeded in subduing them. Wherever he found them congregated together in large villages, he broke them up, burnt the villages and compelled them to dwell on their lands in a number of small hamlets.

In A.D. 1838 some important changes were made by Bunni Singh in the internal administration of the State, and he appointed three clever Mussulmans of Delhi as his Diwans. They were three brothers, the eldest of whom, Ammujun, was the principal. Before the advent of these Diwans, the land revenue of the State had been levied in kind; payments in coin were now substituted. Further, an original attempt was made to establish civil and criminal courts. Notwithstanding these reforms, the Diwans were guilty of many corruptions and intrigues, and it was not till A.D. 1851, that a stupendous embezzlement of the State revenue was discovered. The Diwans were tried and imprisoned; but unfortunately they were subsequently released on paying a heavy fine, and they were not long before they regained their former influence over the Chief and reverted to their own peculiar mode of administering the State.

Bunni Singh in the meanwhile, devoted his time and energies to the construction of palaces, bunds and lakes and to the improvement of irrigation. The most notable of these public works, which exist to the present day, are the City Palace, and the Bunni Bilas Palace; but his great work was undoubtedly the bund, or dam, at Silesergh, about eight miles distant from the Ulwar city. In fact, this great work—due entirely to Bunni Singh—has changed the barren lands which previously surrounded the city into a number of luxuriant gardens.

He was also a patron of arts and letters, and attracted painters and artisans from all parts of India to his service, and he spent large sums of money in the collection of a fine library of oriental works.

During the last five years of his life, he suffered from paralysis, and lost the power of speech, and in other respects was physically unable to control the administration of his State. The Diwans consequently exercised unlimited power.

Just before his death the Indian Mutiny had broken out, and bed-ridden as he was, Bunni Singh in A.D. 1857 selected the flower of his army, and despatched a force, consisting of 800 infantry, 400 cavalry, and four guns, to the assistance of the beleaguered garrison at Agra. Most of the cavalry consisted of the "Khan's Chauki" or the Chief's personal guard who were all Rajputs, the remaining portion of the force were principally Mussulmans. A brigade of mutineers from Nusseerabad came upon this force at Achnera, a town on the road between Bhurtpore and Agra. The Rajput cavalry, loyal to their Chief and the British, were deserted by all the Mussulmans and by their leader Raja Bahadur Chimman Singh (grandson of Samrat Singh Kalianot, one of Purtap Singh's officials). The Rajputs suffered a severe defeat, leaving 55 men killed on the field of battle, amongst whom were ten thakurs of note, whose heirs subsequently received *killats* from the British Government.

When the sad news reached Ulwar, the loyal Chief Bunni Singh was at the point of death ; his reason had fled, and he was spared the sorrowful news. The last order, it is said, he ever gave, in writing, (as he had lost the power of speech,) was that a large sum of money should be sent to his small force.

Bunni Singh died in August 1857, and the sad tale of his death cannot but invoke a feeling of admiration and respect to his memory.

In concluding this chapter, I cannot do better than quote the words of Captain Cadell with reference to the character of this Chief :—" Jealous of power, fond of State ceremony, anxious to be just without sacrificing what he considered his interest at the shrine of justice, at times generous to excess, at others niggardly, kindly dispositioned, but occasionally cruel ; he was on the whole an excellent type of a good native chief of the past generation. His good deeds are remembered, and his bad ones are forgotten by the people."

CHAPTER VI.

LIFE AND SOVEREIGNTY OF HIS HIGHNESS SEWAEE SHEODAN SINGH, MAHA RAO RAJAH OF ULWAR,

4th CHIEF OF THE ULWAR STATE.

Ascended the Gadi A.D. 1857.—*Died A.D.* 1874.

It would be a pleasant task to record that the progress of civil administration, which began in its primitive way during the sovereignty of Bunni Singh, had been continued by Sheodan Singh, but a perusal of the events of his short life gives a direct negative to such an assertion, so far as his own personal control over his dominions is concerned.

At the time of the death of Bunni Singh, Sheodan Singh was a lad, 12 years of age; and as he was the only legitimate son of the late Chief, he succeeded to the *gadi*. This is the first instance in the history of this State in which a legitimate son succeeded his father on the Ulwar *gadi*, all the former Chiefs having been adopted.

The curse and ban of a minority of former days were perhaps never so manifest as in this instance. The Delhi Diwans continued to carry on the administration of the State, and early ingratiated themselves in the good favour of the young Chief over whom they gained great influence. The Rajputs naturally did not appreciate this state of affairs, especially as the Chief shewed his preference for the Mussulmans, and his conduct so exasperated the religious and social feelings of the Rajputs, that they lost all patience with their Chief. In August 1858, the Rajputs, headed by Thakur Lakhdir Singh, collected as many of their clansmen as they could, and a conflict took place between the two factions ; a good deal of blood was shed, and all the Diwans were taken prisoners; and Thakur Lakhdir Singh, a man of fine character, but proud and jealous of his noble race and birth, did all he could to avert further bloodshed by banish-ing the Diwans beyond the limits of the State. He immediately re-ported the occurrence of the disturbance to the British authorities, and it was decided that a Council of Administration should be appointed, with Thakur Lakhdir Singh as President. This measure caused a complete revolution of the previous administration, which had been entirely in the hands of the Mussulman Diwans, . and consequently it was soon evident that the new Council could not cope with the powerful opposition of the young Chief, and his allies. The British authorities then sent a British officer to Ulwar, to con-duct the administration of the State during the minority of the Chief.

With the assistance of a new Council, the administration was thus carried on till A.D. 1863, when the Maha Rao Raja was invested with power. Sheodan Singh consequently had now the complete control of his State.

Soon after his accession, one of his first actions was to order Thakur Lakhdir Singh to retire to his own jagir at Bijwar ; and to further punish him, Sheodan Singh confiscated his village of Bhangrowlee, which was conferred on him by Bunni Singh in A.D. 1858.

When the Mussulman Diwans were expelled from Ulwar, they were banished to Benares, but were allowed to return to Delhi on the understanding that they would have no further communication with Ulwar. On hearing of their return to Delhi, Sheodan Singh immediately took advantage of the occasion, and again entrusted them with the control and management of the State. Former malpractices speedily set in ; almost all the officials at the time were dismissed, and their positions were usurped by Mussulmans.

Seeing that the Mussulmans were again in power in Ulwar, Thakur Lakhdir Singh foolishly invaded Ulwar in A.D. 1866 with a body of his followers, but without success. He was rightly reprimanded for his conduct on this occasion, but was permitted to retire to Jeypore. In 1870 another insurrection broke out, practically between the Rajputs and Mussulmans ; and further, owing to Sheodan Singh's extravagance, combined with the malpractices of the Diwans, it was soon evident that the State was in a condition verging on bankruptcy.

Under the circumstances it was thought expedient, in the best interests of the State, to send a British officer to Ulwar to control the administration of the State.   Naturally, at first, Sheodan Singh resented this policy, but he suffered from ill-health. and was at the time a confirmed invalid, and died in October 1874 of brain fever at a comparatively early age.

CHAPTER VII.

HIS HIGHNESS SEWAEE MUNGAL SINGH, BAHADUR, G. C. S. I., MAHARAJAH OF ULWAR.

HONORARY LIEUTENANT-COLONEL IN THE BRITISH ARMY AND 5TH CHIEF OF THE ULWAR STATE.

Ascended the Gadi A.D. 1874—*Died A.D.* 1892.

In briefly recording the principal events of the short sovereignty of this Chief, it is too evident that its brevity was an unfortunate circumstance for the general welfare of his people. He lived at a time when most rapid progress, in the most literal sense of the word, was taking place, not only in his own State but throughout all the Feudatory States in India, and Mungal Singh was in his best days an excellent example of the modern native ruler. Well educated, shrewd, clever and painstaking, he was at the same time just and upright in his actions. His natural courtesy, good nature and genial disposition made him popular with both Europeans and natives with whom he came in contact, and his death, in the prime of his life, will be long deplored by one and all. His accession to the

(41)

gadi was not devoid of interest, as Sheodan Singh left no legitimate son ; so the doctrine of adoption was applied in his case. Mungal Singh was selected by the " Bara Kotri," and their choice was confirmed by the British Government.

His sovereignty is of too recent date to need a detailed history, but the following events may be noted as constituting, some at least, of the many notable occurrences of his tenure of rule:—His elevation to the G. C. S. I. ; his appointment as an honorary Lieutenant-Colonel in the British Army ; the foundation of a Lady Dufferin Hospital in Ulwar, and his personal interest in assisting to further the objects of the Lady Dufferin Fund ; the opening of new dispensaries in his State ; the formation of a breeding establishment for horses on a large scale : His Highness' willing co-operation and loyalty in establishing and maintaining a Cavalry and an Infantry Regiment in connection with the Imperial Defences : his visit to Australia, as His Highness was the first Chief of note who had ever visited the colonies, &c.

During the latter portion of his life Mungal Singh suffered from failing health, and he died at Naini Tal in May 1892.

He is succeeded by his only son—

HIS HIGHNESS SEWAEE JEY SINGH, BAHADUR,

MAHARAJAH OF ULWAR, AND 6TH CHIEF OF THE ULWAR STATE.

Born A.D. 1881—*Ascended the Gadi A.D.* 1892.

THE ULWAR CHIEFS.

Name.		Birth.	Ascended the *Gadi.*	Death.	Length of Sovereignty.
		A. D.	A. D.	A. D.	
1. Purtap Singh	...	1740	1753	1790	37 years.
2. Bakhtawar Singh	...	1779	1791	1815	24 years.
3. Bunni Singh	...	1808	1815	1857	42 years.
4. Sheodan Singh	...	1845	1857	1874	17 years.
5. Mungal Singh	...	1859	1874	1892	18 years.
6. Jey Singh	...	1881	1892	...	...

www.ingramcontent.com/pod-product-compliance
Lightning Source LLC
Chambersburg PA
CBHW031819090426
42739CB00008B/1336